CRACKS

Jane Ellen Glasser

FUTURECYCLE PRESS

www.futurecycle.org

Cover artwork, "Mona Lisa," by Leonardo da Vinci; author photo by Lenny Gayle; cover and interior book design by Diane Kistner; Book Antiqua text and titling

Published by FutureCycle Press
Lexington, Kentucky, USA

ISBN 978-1-938853-79-1

Contents

Soloist..7

Huis Clos..8

What She Longed For..9

For the Love of Certain Spaces..10

Eden Cottage..11

One Apple..12

Daphne's Plea..13

On Happiness..14

Constitutional..15

Housekeeping According to a Yogini..................................16

Cracks..17

Turkey Buzzards..18

The Mating..19

Rumination on Romantic Love..20

How We Happened..21

Good Intentions..22

Now That I Am Old..23

Arguments Against a Hearing Aid......................................24

Commuters..25

Winter's Lessons..26

Still Life in Blue..27

Bedtime Imperative..28

Bella Donna..29

Last Wishes..30

Acknowledgments

For Hara, my finest creation

There is a crack in everything; that's how the light gets in.

— Leonard Cohen

When the Japanese mend broken objects, they aggrandize the damage by filling the cracks with gold. They believe that when something's suffered damage and has a history, it becomes more beautiful.

— Billie Mobayed

Soloist

Like an ornament
at the apex of a clay roof,
a single bird will perch,
lord of the highest view.

This morning it's a dove
dissolving against the soft
grey of an overcast sky.
Better than high branches

or high wires, here he is
a soloist, rooster of the skies,
loosening his six-note aria
on the empty street below.

From my open window
in an adjacent building,
I sit watching, listening
to his abandoned heart,

thinking, this is the way
a poem writes itself,
note by solitary note
on the prevailing air.

Huis Clos

After *The Joy of Life* by Paul Delvaux

In the clutch of what could have been
a slow dance, the couple are like boats
moored in the same berth
on a windless day.

Her hand will never leave the blue
mesa of his shoulder, his right arm
will never slip below her waist.

He will never feel her breath
on his neck, inhale her perfume,
or taste the red fruit of her lips.

Their legs will never rub against each other,
igniting a fire, because
it is impossible to dance in a painting.

Though the canvas holds a ballroom,
the world ends at its corners.

This is the torment Sartre warned about:
Stalled in one place forever, a breath away
from everything you have ever wished for.

What She Longed For

To slip out of her past
the way an unzipped dress
puddles to the floor;

to empty the mind
and feel it flap
like a windsock;

to let spirit play,
dust motes
on ladders of light;

to set her senses
singing
through all her organs;

to dance
across continents
while standing still.

For the Love of Certain Spaces

The moon's watermark
on a brightening sky,
highways that fall away
to the horizon, a dirt trail
beneath arched trees,
avenues lined in the airy
giants of Australian pines,
woodlands glazed in ice,
a roadside intoxicated
with poppies, wetlands
crowned with duckweed
and the yellow fists
of spatterdock, islands
tremulous with wings,
a shoreline's give and take
over which a pelican
pulls a string of pelicans,
the fifty blues of the ocean,
a solitary cabin beside
a scribbling stream,
the black snake
of a mountain pass,
a cave's musky breath,
dusk's descending veils,
on an evening flight
from 3,000 feet
the fallen constellations
of city lights, pressing
down in the pure dark
of the countryside
the brilliant stars.

Eden Cottage

Charlottesville, VA

Over clay and blue stone
the creek's song keeps going
thin in its dry throat.

The morning-wet grass
is seeded with sound,
a muted unwinding of gears.

Green backed with green
deepens in shadow.
Wind rustle. Bird chatter.

Now sound transmutes
into motion, as if song,
internalized, fuels the wings.

A goldfinch lasers
a trajectory, hickory to feeder.
The air hums like a taut wire.

Beyond, July's uncut fields
dance to a reel that skirts
the registers of the human ear.

One Apple

Why claim the whole orchard
or even one tree bowed
with fruit, at its base
a devil of bees feasting?

One is enough for a treatise
on beauty, sin, and death.
What else could tell us
so much about ourselves,

we who were schooled by Eve,
a queen proffering poison,
the worm. Just one granted
access to the Elysian Fields,
slammed Eden's Gates.

Cezanne swore he'd astonish
Paris with an apple, and he did.

Daphne's Plea

Help me, Father! Open the earth
to enclose me, or change my form.

I refuse to trade my woodlands
for the tomb of a marriage house.

Don't speak to me of grandchildren!

Bobolinks sing lullabies sweeter than I
who would rather romp barefoot
with the rabbit and the red fox

than be cracked open like a mollusk
to let Apollo in. These hips
were not meant to dandle babies.

Keep me safe, Father,
from the hard wants of a man.

If I must be rooted, plant my feet
in rich soil, let my womanly flesh
harden to bark, and let my limbs,

robust in sleeves of evergreen,
keep reaching for the sun.

On Happiness

A white boat plowing,
the prow lifting and lifting
where two black Labs
lean out, drinking
the rush of windspray,
the man behind them,
his hair alive as wings,
his lips thrown back,
steering yet relinquishing
himself to something greater
than this bend of river,
his little boat, his two dogs.

Constitutional

Foxtail fronds
sweep the sky
not a cloud
drifting
a spilling
sun lacquering
trees
cars
the Spanish tile
of rooftops
like a shook rug
a flapping flag
its cord singing
on metal
now
and again
a few solitary
birds
blown east
the wind's
hand
at my back

Housekeeping According to a Yogini

Inhale
and the household
gods enter,
waving brooms and mops,
carrying buckets
of lemon-scented Joy.

Drunk on letting go,
they exhale
past and future,

confiscate newspapers,
money, mirrors,
sweep and scrub and dust

until the air inside
is so pure
the I that no longer exists
begs to stay forever.

Cracks

If you look closely,
Mona Lisa's lips
are chapped
with cracks.

In Rilke's elegy,
death zigzags
on a china cup.

Don't give me
perfection
immune to clocks.

Don't give me
the unbroken,
the safely stored
in airless vaults.

Every scar
is the shorthand
of an important story.

Each crack
is a door opening
onto a larger room.

Turkey Buzzards

Wings uplifted in a V,
they soar in wobbly circles,
riding thermals
to scan the countryside;

or, steered by smell,
they glide low,
their shadows gracing
pastures, dumpsters,
the black tablecloths
of highways.

A fresh kill
will draw a wake,
bald heads bobbing,
hooked bills tearing
into any sick
or breathless thing.

At night they retreat
to the skeletons of trees,
their only song a dirge
of grunts and hisses.

The Mating

In the expectant stillness
of dance partners,
they face each other,
tuned to an
inner music
that sets their heads
pumping, pumping,
his tail shaking
like a happy dog's,
till in one precise
movement
he mounts,
pounces really,
his gleaming body
in full vibrato;
then, in a blink,
he's off
circling her,
his wake
like an echo
widening out
from the cove's heart.

Rumination on Romantic Love

Romance refuses to sleep
its life away in the same bed.

When the storm hushes
and the landscape droops
to a tedious calm,
the heart plots its escape.

So we learn from Shakespeare,
Kierkegaard, Flaubert.

At the death of her affairs,
Madame Bovary chose arsenic —
antidote to a mediocre life.

Ophelia went mad. Juliet died
twice. I slough the past, waking
with windows thrown wide —

some days in the arms of love,
some days alone.

How We Happened

You arrived like a letter forwarded to a wrong address,
like a dog's nose to the ground seeking its way home,
like the last peach on a tree, or a stone skipped across
water to land safely in the palm of a leaf. You came

out of a seeming nowhere like a slow-developing sheet
of film; like a fledgling, fanning the air from the lip
of its nest; like the sun, at day's end, content to bleed
into a purpled horizon. Like a bet decided on the flip

of a coin, *Heads,* you called. And I answered, the way
mourning doves volley songs through a stand of pines,
a bounced ball returns to a child's hand, or a stray
shadows a boy's heart to a door. Like a trumpet vine

to a hummingbird, I invited you in. *Stay!* I said,
Stay like a rock washed smooth by a river. And you did.

Good Intentions

Pear trees burst into blossom.
Sun sparkles off the blue Fiesta
he no longer drives. His neighbor

is out walking his dog. Stop. Start.
Stop. A dog believes he owns
his street and must sniff

before signing the right spot.
The man has grown used to living
alone. Everything he touches—

door knobs, banister, a spoon—
had been touched years ago
by his wife and children. And yet

he feels the loss; the days keep
falling into a black river.
He is careful not to mention this.

Yesterday, his two sons brought
picturesque brochures, good
intentions. He can still bake

a chicken on Sunday and make
it last the week. He remembers
his pills. The April air is redolent.

After breakfast, he will work
in the garden, clear weeds
from the emerging daffodils.

Now That I Am Old

I am no longer afraid
of shadows,
snapping teeth,
the clap and slash
of split skies,
prayers unanswered
for the soul's keep.

I am no longer afraid
of being loved
or not being loved.

I am no longer afraid
of what has no face:
pestilence, floods,
nuclear bombs.

No one escapes
the indifferent flame,
earth's hunger.

Open the gates
of the asylum, the prison.
I will take my chances.

But you,
innocent one,
who sits smiling
at the beating
of sorrow's dog,
of you I am afraid.

Arguments Against a Hearing Aid

I have no difficulty carrying on conversations
with myself. In dreams my hearing's perfect.

There's more room for silence — that stilled pond
upon which my best thoughts float.

Never one for idle talk, I get by with a head shake
and a smile. Eventually eyes, those quick learners,

pick up a second language. As for the world,
despair is a bottom feeder; it cups its ear

to bad news. Every day I decrease the number
of war dead, starving children, natural disasters.

I keep telling myself, you'll never miss
the dance of squirrels mornings on the tin roof;

behind the house, the kiss of the kingfisher
puncturing a hole in the Lafayette River;

the plucked heart of a Brahms concerto;
the vespers of birdsong in the pines.

Commuters

For this brief ride,
this bridge between
clocked time,
they place their cares
in the passenger seat.

Soon they will enter
well-lit rooms where
stocks rise or dip
and bombs burst
in foreign cities.

If there is a family,
a dinner waiting,
this, too, will need
work. For now,

the sun sputtering
on the horizon,
their lives set
on cruise control,

they lean into the dark.

Winter's Lessons

Trees stripped of summer's store
and fall's giveaway reveal the bones
of what stays. The river frozen

to the shore's lip speaks less,
keeps to itself what belongs to itself.
The bear in his den, the bat suspended

in his cave, know when to sleep
and when to wake. No longer
hitched to the world's rhythms,

no longer ruled by appetite, they wait
for an inner pull to rouse them.
And what is more instructional

than snowfall, its knack for making
the familiar new? Or night, arriving early,
flooding its borders at both ends?

Still Life in Blue

After *Difficult Child* by Lisa Hess Hesselgrave

Nothing is happening in the world of her room.
The ivories lie still as teeth in a jar. Yesterday
she played a lively toccata, her hands dancing
the keys. Today she sits, hands in lap like a child
waiting to be told when to lift the fork and eat.

The table is bare, her shadow staining its white cloth.
Is she waiting for something, a ring, a knock, to break
the spell that keeps her frozen in the hard-backed chair?
Perhaps she has disappeared into prayer, her thoughts
impervious to time as an hourglass drained of sand.

Maybe this is what death would feel like —
a featureless globe atop a mute piano,
a strapless gown for shroud, and you, forever
going nowhere in the coffin of a blue room.

Bedtime Imperative

Turn off the TV.
Turn off the lights.

Open the windows.
Open your hinged heart.

Let night enter,
black-faced, spilling
moonlight across the floor.

Turn down the covers.

Turn down the voice
of the caviller in your head.

Let go of your age.
Let go of lists.

Rejoice in the gift
of cool sheets.

Rejoice in the respite
of an unmanned skiff
adrift on a lake
strewn with stars.

Close your eyes.

Let curtains fall.
Let curtains rise.

Bella Donna

After *Resting Somnambulist IV* by Pyke Koch

Let the candle go out.
Put the sewing machine to bed.
Do not worry. When you wake,

sunlight will stitch the world back
to a motley quilt. Relax

as your mattress greens
with nightshade's leaves.

Feel yourself fall
into a delirium
beneath a chuppah of stars.

Bella Donna, here in this dream,
on this plain of death,
know you are truly alive.

Last Wishes

As I contrived a life
out of the box,
scatter my death
on the wind's back.

Let me live again
to mine the earth
in the belly of a worm.

For dirge, rain
on a tin roof,
a dog's yelp,
the laughter of leaves.

No make-up,
no touched-up
script for eulogy.

Say I was happily flawed.
Say I was human.

Acknowledgments

I am grateful to the editors of the journals in which these poems, several in different form, first appeared.

Avatar 16: "Now That I Am Old," "Still Life in Blue"
Goodreads Newsletter July 2013: "Daphne's Plea"
Innisfree 17: "What She Longed For," "Winter's Lessons"
Letters, March 8 2013 in "Writing My Own Obituary"
     by John Siegfried: "Last Wishes"
Minerva Rising 5: "Bella Donna"
Passager: "Arguments Against a Hearing Aid"
Silver Blade 22: "For the Love of Certain Spaces,"
     "How We Happened"

The following poems received awards:

"Huis Clos," second-place finalist, May 2014 *Goodreads Newsletter* Poetry Contest; "Daphne's Plea," winner, July 2013 *Goodreads Newsletter* Poetry Contest; "Winter's Lessons," first honorable mention, Emma Triss Memorial, Poetry Society of VA; "Good Intentions," second honorable mention, Joe Pendleton Campbell Memorial, Poetry Society of VA; "Bedtime Imperative," winner, Broward County South Regional Poetry Contest

I am indebted to Mary McCue and Mary-Jean Kledzik for their review of this manuscript and their ongoing critical feedback of my work. I am grateful to Jon Frangipane, Wendell Abern, and all the members of the Fort Lauderdale Writers' Group for their invaluable support.

About FutureCycle Press

FutureCycle Press is dedicated to publishing lasting English-language poetry books, chapbooks, and anthologies in both print-on-demand and ebook formats. Founded in 2007 by long-time independent editor/publishers and partners Diane Kistner and Robert S. King, the press incorporated as a non-profit in 2012. A number of our editors are distinguished poets and writers in their own right, and we have been actively involved in the small press movement going back to the early seventies.

The FutureCycle Poetry Book Prize and honorarium is awarded annually for the best full-length volume of poetry we publish in a calendar year. Introduced in 2013, our Good Works projects are anthologies devoted to issues of universal significance, with all proceeds donated to a related worthy cause. Our Selected Poems series highlights contemporary poets with a substantial body of work to their credit; with this series we strive to resurrect work that has had limited distribution and is now out of print.

We are dedicated to giving all of the authors we publish the care their work deserves, making our catalog of titles the most diverse and distinguished it can be, and paying forward any earnings to fund more great books.

We've learned a few things about publishing over the years. We've also evolved a unique, resilient publishing model that allows us to focus mainly on vetting and preserving for posterity the most books of exceptional quality without becoming overwhelmed with bookkeeping and mailing, fund-raising activities, or taxing editorial and production "bubbles." To find out more about what we are doing, come see us at www.futurecycle.org.